BUSES AND COACHES IN SOUTH EAST WALES IN THE 1970s

MIKE STREET

AMBERLEY

First published 2019

Amberley Publishing
The Hill, Stroud
Gloucestershire, GL5 4EP

www.amberley-books.com

Copyright © Mike Street, 2019

The right of Mike Street to be identified as
the Author of this work has been asserted in
accordance with the Copyrights, Designs and
Patents Act 1988.

ISBN 978 1 4456 9006 3 (print)
ISBN 978 1 4456 9007 0 (ebook)

British Library Cataloguing in Publication Data.
A catalogue record for this book is available from
the British Library.

Origination by Amberley Publishing.
Printed in the UK.

Intoduction

The Author

I have lived in Cardiff since my birth in 1953. My interest in buses started in 1965 when a classmate at high school produced a copy of Ian Allan's *British Bus Fleets* book. Photography followed in 1968, firstly in black and white, followed by colour slide, then colour print and finally digital from 2002. After a thirty-three-year career in local government (finance and IT, not transport!), early retirement in 2004 gave me the opportunity to commence scanning the 20,000 plus photographs I have taken over the years.

When I started photographing buses I tended to concentrate on the major operators and new vehicles of the smaller operators. One Sunday when photographing in the coach park at Porthcawl I was accosted by a driver who wanted to know why I didn't photograph his coach. I said that I was not interested in the older vehicles, just the newer ones. His reply was that the newer ones would be there next year, but the older ones could have been sold on or even gone for scrap and then I would have missed them. I took his words to heart and just wish I'd also started to photograph the minibuses that were around at the time!

Although this book concentrates on the 1970s, some images from my earliest days of 35 mm photography in 1968/9 are included. The selection of photographs is very much a personal one, though I have tried to include a broad cross section of operators and vehicle types, the emphasis being on the smaller, independent operators rather than the municipal and National Bus Company operators.

The Area

I regard South East Wales as being the pre-1974 Local Government Reorganisation counties of Monmouthshire to the east and Glamorganshire to the west (and the parts of surrounding counties gained in 1974). Simplistically, the April 1974 Reorganisation saw Monmouthshire become the county of Gwent, gaining the area around Brynmawr from Brecknockshire but losing the Rhymney Valley to Mid Glamorgan, while Glamorganshire was split into three parts: Mid Glamorgan comprising the eastern and northern parts, including Aberdare, Bridgend, Caerphilly, Merthyr Tydfil and Pontypridd; South Glamorgan comprising the area around Cardiff and the Vale of Glamorgan; and West Glamorgan comprising the area around the city of Swansea, Neath and Port Talbot. Beneath these new counties, the previous structure of County Brough Councils (CBC), Urban District Councils (UDC) and Rural District Councils (RDC) was replaced by Borough Councils (BC) or District Councils (DC). Wales succumbed to another Local Government Reorganisation in April 1996 when the counties and districts were replaced by unitary authorities, but that is beyond the scope of this book.

The Major Operators

In 1968 the councils at Aberdare, Bedwas & Machen, Caerphilly, Cardiff, Gelligaer, Merthyr Tydfil, Newport, Pontypridd and Bedwellty & Mynyddislwyn (as the West Monmouthshire Omnibus Board) were running bus fleets. The 1974 Local Government Reorganisation saw Aberdare UDC become part of Cynon Valley Borough Council, the UDCs of Bedwas & Machen, Caerphilly and Gelligaer merge as part of Rhymney Valley District Council, Pontypridd UDC become part of Taff-Ely Borough Council and the West Mon Omnibus Board become part of Islwyn Borough Council. Control of the larger County Borough Council fleets of Cardiff, Merthyr Tydfil and Newport remained unchanged.

March 1968 saw the British Electric Traction Company selling its bus interests to the state, a move which would see a merger between its fleets and those of the nationalised Transport Holding Company to form the National Bus Company on 1 January 1969. BET fleets in the area were Neath & Cardiff Luxury Coaches Ltd, The Rhondda Transport Company Ltd, The South Wales Transport Company Ltd, Thomas Bros (Port Talbot) Ltd and the Western Welsh Omnibus Company Ltd. The THC fleets were Red & White Services Ltd and United Welsh Services Ltd.

The newly formed National Bus Company acquired Jones Omnibus Services Ltd of Aberbeg in April 1969 and placed it under the overall management of Red & White. Rationalisation of the National Bus Company fleets also started in April 1969 when South Wales Transport gained control of Neath & Cardiff and Thomas Bros, followed in September 1970 by control of United Welsh; the three fleets were completely absorbed in January 1971. In the east, Western Welsh absorbed Rhondda Transport Co. in January 1971. In 1972 the operations of Western Welsh were curtailed to the area east of Pyle, with Neath Abbey depot and services being transferred to South Wales Transport in January and Haverfordwest at the end of March. The operations at Newcastle Emlyn, Lampeter (outstation) and New Quay passed from Western Welsh to Crosville Motor Services in April 1972. Although remaining separate companies, the managerial functions of Western Welsh, Red & White and Jones were fully merged from October 1974. Control of Red & White passed to Western Welsh in January 1978 and Western Welsh was renamed National Welsh Omnibus Services Ltd that April. Finally, the vehicles and services of Jones passed to National Welsh in January 1981.

The Independent Operators

In 1973 there were sixteen operators in Cardiff, six in Merthyr Tydfil, fifteen in Newport and twelve in Swansea with the rest of Glamorgan hosting 128 and Monmouthshire seventy-six. The majority of operators had just a handful of vehicles and the only ones with twenty or more were Morlais Services, Merthyr Tydfil (twenty-four); D. Davies (D Coaches), Morriston (thirty-two); Morris Bros, Swansea (fifty-seven); Brewer, Caerau (twenty-seven); Cream Line, Tonmawr (twenty-nine); Jenkins, Skewen (twenty-one); Llynfi, Maesteg (thirty-six); Contract Bus Services, Caerwent (seventy-one); R. I. Davies, Tredegar (twenty-seven); and Hill's, Tredegar (forty-five). R. I. Davies and Hill's were early operators of continental holidays and had luxury coach fleets for that work; R. I. Davies was also one of the first operators in the area to purchase foreign coachwork, from Van Hool of Belgium.

Many of the operators ran schools services and works services (often using elderly double-deckers) to the collieries and to industrial estates which had been opened on the sites of wartime munitions factories. Contract Bus Services was unique in being the transport arm of the major civil engineering and building contractor Sir Robert McAlpine and its vehicles were used solely as works transport to and from their sites. By 1979 Morlais Services and R. I. Davies had ceased and Contract Bus Services had reverted to non-PSV status. Fleets which had expanded to over twenty vehicles included S. A. Bebb, Llantwit Fardre (now twenty-four vehicles); Cleverly (Capitol Coaches), Pontypool (forty-nine); Hopkins, Tonna (thirty); Bryn Morgan, Monmouth (twenty-two); and Morris Travel, Pencoed (twenty-two). With deregulation in the 1980s considerable changes both to operators and services took place, but that story is for another day.

The Vehicles

By 1968 the half-cab coach was quite a rarity in this area, most operators running lightweight Bedford and Ford vehicles; however, Aberdare, Bedwas & Machen, Caerphilly, Gelligaer and Pontypridd Urban District Councils were still running half-cab single-deck buses. I was lucky enough to photograph examples of the AEC Monocoach, Regal III and IV, Albion Aberdonian and Nimbus, Bedford OB, Bristol K, BUT 9641T, Commer Avenger I and IV, Crossley DD42, Daimler Roadliner (a modern but rather unsuccessful vehicle), Guy Arab III and Leyland Tiger PS1, and some of these photographs appear in this book. Despite the preponderance of Bedford and Ford coaches with Duple and Plaxton coachwork I have endeavoured to include a broad cross section of the vehicles in use in the 1970s.

The Locations

Cardiff hosted Five Nations (as it then was) Rugby Union fixtures in the spring and the annual South Wales Miners' Gala in June; these events meant a large number of coaches parked up around the city centre and nearby Sophia Gardens. Summer Sunday afternoons would often see a family trip to Porthcawl or, less frequently, Aberavon or Barry Island. At these locations it would not be unusual to find upwards of thirty coaches and, quite often, double-deckers from The Rhondda Transport Co. running private hires from the Working Men's and Non-Political Clubs in the South Wales valleys. Other trips were made with older friends who had their own cars at the time; locations visited included Newport, Caerphilly, Pontypridd, Merthyr Tydfil, etc., and some 'out-of-the-way' places such as Maesteg, Skewen and Tonmawr.

Acknowledgements

Firstly, my thanks to the operators and their staff who, almost fifty years ago, were willing to allow entry to their depots to photograph the buses and coaches – something very rarely possible these days following the introduction of Health & Safety regulations. Secondly, thanks to my older friends (especially Allan, Mac and Roger) for the trips out to take photographs in the days before I had my own transport, and also to my late parents, Pam and Dennis, for the Sunday outings with a similar goal. Acknowledgement is also due to the PSV Circle, whose publications have proved invaluable in researching the details and histories of the vehicles, and to various online sites which have filled in many gaps in my knowledge. Thanks also to Connor Stait at Amberley Publishing for the suggestion that I write this book and to the staff at Amberley for organising it into a publishable format. Finally, thanks to my wife, Carole, and mother-in-law, Betty, for putting up with my endless hours on the computer scanning slides and negatives. In conclusion, any errors in this publication are mine, and mine alone!

Mike Street
Cardiff
January 2019

Municipal (Council) Fleets

Four Guy Arab III 6LWs fitted with Northern Counties B35R bodywork entered the Aberdare UDC fleet in 1951. At this time most collieries did not have pithead baths, so the buses were fitted with wooden slatted seats. 11 (LNY 854) was seen at the Gadlys depot in August 1969; it went for scrap in May 1972.

Aberdare UDC bought five Guy Arab IV 6LW chassis in 1958 and had them bodied by Longwell Green on Metal Sections framework as H35/29R double-deckers. 55 (XNY 411) was caught in Cardiff Street in its home town in March 1972. It was withdrawn later the same year.

Aberdare UDC 83 (XDW 983K), a Commer KCBN3023 with a Rootes B15F body, replaced a 1962 Morris LDO5 in 1972. Photographed at the depot in April 1973, it passed to Cynon Valley BC in April 1974 and was sold in June 1980.

Bedwas & Machen UDC 7 (JWO 355), a 1951 AEC Regal III 9621A with a Bruce Coach Works B35R body, is flanked by Gelligaer UDC 19 (MTG 884), a 1953 AEC Regal III 9621A with a Longwell Green B35F body, and Caerphilly UDC 51 (LTX 311), a 1952 Leyland Tiger PS2/5 with a Massey B35F body, at Caerphilly's Mill Road depot on 31 March 1974. At this time the Bedwas & Machen and Gelligaer vehicles were in preservation and the Caerphilly bus was a driver trainer. The following day the three operators would become part of the new Rhymney Valley District Council.

Bedwas & Machen UDC 8 (BWO 585B), a 1964 Massey L31/28R-bodied AEC Regent V 2MD3RA, was seen at the depot in May 1973. It passed to Rhymney Valley DC in April 1974 as fleet number 92. It was sold in April 1979 and is currently preserved.

Caerphilly UDC 29 (557 MNY) carried this experimental livery for a short time in 1969; it was a Leyland Titan PD3/4 with a Massey L35/33R body and was new in November 1961. Caught in Cardiff bus station in September 1969, it passed to Rhymney Valley DC in April 1974 but was withdrawn and dismantled for spares later that year.

Caerphilly UDC 13 (13 SNY) was a Leyland Leopard PSU3/1R with a Massey B55F body new in July 1963; the sliding driver's door was unusual on underfloor-engined single-deckers. Seen at Mill Road depot on 31 March 1974, it passed to Rhymney Valley DC the following day; withdrawn in May 1978, it was dismantled for spares.

Caerphilly UDC bought 48 (ETG 48K), a Commer PB with a Rootes twelve-seat minibus body, in November 1971 to replace a 1963 Austin JO2. Photographed at its Mill Road depot in May 1973, it became Rhymney Valley DC 25 in April 1974 and was later used for staff transport.

Delivered to Caerphilly UDC in October 1973, 40 (NUH 40M) was a Leyland Atlantean AN68/1R with East Lancs H45/33F bodywork. Photographed on 31 March 1974, it survived with Rhymney Valley DC until August 1986.

The Cardiff trolleybus system lasted until January 1970 and here we see number 216 (DBO 476), a 1948 BUT 9641T with an East Lancs H38/29R body, rounding The Monument on its approach to the St Mary Street terminus of service 1 from Gabalfa on Wednesday 24 April 1968. The route was converted to motorbus operation the following weekend.

Cardiff 46 (EBO 900) was a 1949 Crossley DD42/7 with Alexander L27/26R bodywork to Leyland design. It passed to the Cardiff 46 Group for preservation in 1966 and, for a time, was used on various day trips. Here it is seen in Abergavenny in September 1972. The slogan on the side refers to its appearance in the Cardiff Lord Mayor's parade earlier in the year.

By 1977 the appearance of a rear-entrance bus on the long Cardiff to Tredegar route was a rarity, but here we see Cardiff's 1966 Guy Arab V 468 (EUH 468D) with an Alexander H37/28R body in Tredegar bus station in July of that year. The Guy Arab V had been designed for 30-foot front-entrance bodywork, so Cardiff was unique in the UK in having 27-foot rear-entrance examples, such as 468.

The last vehicles delivered to Cardiff in the traditional crimson lake and cream livery were 551–85 (WUH 551–85K) at the end of 1971. They were Daimler Fleetline CRL6-30s with Metro-Cammell H43/31F bodywork. Here, the first of the batch is seen in Cardiff bus station in December 1973.

Following Fleetlines 551–85, Cardiff switched to the Bristol VRT for its double-deck requirements. The first batch was 586–605 (PKG 586–605M), VRT/SL6Gs with ECW H41/31F bodywork delivered at the end of 1973. By August 1979 587 (PKG 587M) was carrying this advertising livery for Belle Vue Discount Store. At the time it was rumoured that this vehicle was repainted in error for Fleetline 578 as the VRTs were very rarely used on the route through Blackwood to Tredegar.

Longwell Green B44F-bodied AEC Reliance 2MU3RV 363 MTG was new to
Gelligaer UDC as fleet number 29 in November 1961 and was renumbered 24 in July
1966. Seen at Hanbury Square, Bargoed, in November 1973, it carries the later livery
with white replacing grey. Passing to Rhymney Valley DC as fleet number 63 in April
1974, it was dismantled for spares in early 1976.

The first Bristol VRs to enter service with a south Wales fleet were Gelligaer UDCs
39–41 (BTX 539-41J) in April 1971. They had the Mark 2 VRTSL6LX chassis and
Northern Counties H44/33F bodies. 41 (BTX 541J) is seen outside the Tiryberth
depot in November 1972 on the long route 150 from Rhymney Bridge to Newport,
which was operated jointly with Bedwas & Machen UDC and Red & White.

Despite only having around thirty buses, Gelligaer UDC branched out into coaching in 1973. The second coach bought new, in December 1973, was 103 (RTG 221M), a Bedford YRT with a Duple Dominant Express C53F body which passed to Rhymney Valley DC in April 1974. The new fleet number, 87, can just be seen below the windscreen in this 31 March 1974 view.

Merthyr Tydfil CBC 72 (HB 8336) was one of a pair of Leyland Titan PD2/12s with D. J. Davies H32/28R bodies new in July 1955, around the time that the bodybuilder moved to Treforest Industrial Estate and the corporation acquired the Nantygwenith Street site for its new bus depot. 72 was seen at the depot in August 1969 and was sold to the dealer Bill Way at Cardiff's East Dock in October 1971.

Merthyr Tydfil started a new series of fleet numbers, from 100, for 30-foot-long vehicles in 1958. 105 (HB 9841) was a Leyland Titan PD3/4 with East Lancs H41/32RD bodywork, and was one of a pair (104/5) fitted with platform doors for use on the Merthyr to Cardiff service. It passed to Lancaster City Council in 1974 and was later used as a driver trainer.

Merthyr Tydfil bought two Metro-Scania BR111MHs with B44F bodies in 1973. 186 (KHB 186L), the first of the pair, was seen in Cardiff bus station in March 1974. Unsuccessful in Merthyr, the pair were sold when only five years old. 186 then saw a further seven years' service with Leicester City Transport, which had a large fleet of this type.

Another unsuccessful type in the Merthyr Tydfil fleet was the six Marshall Camair 80-bodied Dennis Dominators bought in 1979, 215–20 (CKG 215–20V), which were again sold after around five years' service. 220 (CKG 220V) was caught in Merthyr's bus station when new in October 1979.

Newport Corporation 154 (NDW 605) was a 1957 Daimler CVG6 with a Longwell Green H33/28R body built on Metal Sections framework. Seen in Newport's High Street in August 1970, it went to Paul Sykes of Barnsley in May 1971 and was, presumably, scrapped.

One of nine Alexander H43/31F-bodied Leyland Atlantean PDR1A/1s delivered to Newport Corporation in 1969, 91 (MDW 391G) was seen at the old Dock Street bus station in August 1973. It was withdrawn in June 1981.

In 1971/2, Newport bought forty-four Metro-Scania BR111MH single-deckers with B40D bodywork. 32 (VDW 432K) is seen entering Commercial Street in August 1973; it lasted in the fleet until December 1984.

In 1957 Pontypridd UDC bought three Guy Arab LUF chassis with unusual Roe forty-one-seat rear-entrance bodies. The middle one of the three, 78 (VNY 656), was seen in the town's bus station in January 1972; it was sold a year later.

A line-up of AEC Regent Vs and Roe-bodied Guy Arab IVs at Pontypridd UDC's Glyntaff depot in May 1973. 87/8 (872/3 MTG), new in 1962, had the less common Johannesburg front. The three vehicles in lighter blue show the new livery introduced in 1971.

Entering service with Pontypridd UDC in January 1966, AEC Regent V 2MD3RAs 93/4 (GTX 936/7D) had the last PSV bodies to be built by Longwell Green of Bristol. 93 was caught at the Glyntaff depot in May 1973.

New to Taff-Ely BC in May 1977, Leyland-National 11351A/1R 25 (RBO 25R) was caught loading in Taff Street, Pontypridd, in September 1977. It passed to National Welsh as fleet number N656 in November 1988 and was delicensed in December 1991.

Ordered by Caerphilly UDC, but delivered after Reorganisation, Rhymney Valley DC's 21 (HHB 48N) was a Leyland Atlantean AN68/1R with an East Lancs H44/33F body new in April 1975. Loaned to City of Cardiff Transport in October 1977, it was seen on service 32 to St Fagans. It lasted (with Inter Valley Link) to pass to National Welsh in April 1989.

Rhymney Valley DC 60 (GTX 360N), a Bristol RESL6G with ECW B47F bodywork, was ordered by Gelligaer UDC but delivered in January 1975 after Reorganisation. Seen in Hanbury Square, Bargoed, in September 1975, the cream and gold fleet name on the cream band is illegible.

The West Monmouthshire Omnibus Board bought 20 (JBO 118), a 1954 Leyland Tiger Cub PSUC1/1 with Weymann B44F bodywork, from Western Welsh in 1967 to replace ex-demonstrator AEC Monocoach NLP 635. It was seen, out of use, at the Blackwood depot in November 1972.

Photographed on the same day as JBO 118 was its replacement in the West Mon fleet: GAX 570L, a Willowbrook B53F-bodied Leyland Leopard PSU3B/2R. It lasted with successor operator Islwyn Borough Transport until 1987.

National Bus Company Fleets

In 1957 Jones of Aberbeeg bought 78 (RAX 714), a Leyland Tiger Cub PSUC1/1T which carried a Weymann B44F body. Photographed entering Newport's Dock Street bus station in October 1969, it was dismantled for spares in May 1970.

The first Jones bus to be repainted in NBC blue livery was 1962 AEC Reliance 2MU3RA 98 EAX, which carried a Willowbrook B45F body. Numbered 110 when new, it had become U3062 when seen at the Aberbeeg depot in April 1975. Renumbered U6562 later in the year, it was sold to the dealer North at Sherburn in 1976.

Jones of Aberbeeg's 122 (FAX 314C) was a rarity, being one of only six Bedford VAL14s bodied by Weymann with its Topaz II coach body. It had been ordered by H. R. Richmond of Epsom as 536 LOR, but entered service with Jones in May 1965. It was sold to Davies of Glyn Neath in August 1971.

The horizontal aluminium strips on its Burlingham C41C body show that 1958 AEC Reliance MU3RV 3282 WB had been new to Sheffield United Tours; it passed to Neath & Cardiff Luxury Coaches Ltd in November 1966 for replacement of the Guy Arab LUF coaches. Painted in N&C's standard brown and red livery, it was seen in Cardiff's Central Square in August 1968, two months before it was withdrawn.

RAX 1G was a Bristol RELL6L with an ECW B53F body and had been new to Red & White as R168 in December 1968. When seen at Ross-on-Wye in August 1980, however, it was with National Welsh. Renumbered R1324 in January 1983, it passed to Gwent Community Services in July of that year.

Originally Red & White N575, GHB 688N was a Leyland National 11351/1R B52F new in March 1975. It passed to National Welsh in 1978 and was seen in Hereford bus station in 1980.

Leyland Leopard PSU3/4RT EHD 522F had an Alexander Y-type C45F body; it had been new to Yorkshire Woollen as 407 in April 1968 but arrived with Western Welsh from National Travel (West) in April 1978. It then became National Welsh UC6768 later that month. It went to dealer C. F. Booth at Rotherham in March 1979.

Red & White bought twenty-nine Bristol LS6Gs with ECW B45F bodywork in 1954, the last of which was U2954 (MAX 129), which entered service that December. Photographed in Monmouth bus station in August 1969, it shows a destination of Wyesham, which is just a short trip to the other side of the River Wye.

The ECW coach body fitted to the Bristol MW6G chassis in the early 1960s produced a handsome combination. Red & White UC263 (24 FAX), a thirty-nine-seat example, was actually new in December 1962 and was seen on its way to Cardiff's bus station in July 1969. Renumbered UC5863 in 1975, it was sold in September 1976.

Red & White R565 (GAX 5C) was a Bristol RELL6G with ECW B54F bodywork and was new in October 1965. It was seen in Cinderford in October 1972, just after being repainted in NBC livery, but note the non-standard fleet number on the front and black lining-out to the white band!

Red & White's 1973 Bristol RELH6Ls RC2–573 (NAX 3–6M), with Plaxton Elite Express C47F bodies, were the first coaches delivered in the National Bus Company's white coach livery. RC473 (NAX 5M) is seen in Cardiff bus station during September 1973, its first month in service.

Delivered to the Rhondda Transport Co. as 454 in 1961, AEC Regent V 2D3RA 454 KTG had a Metro-Cammell H39/31F body. It passed to Western Welsh in January 1971, but was still carrying Rhondda fleet names that December. Sold to the Kowloon Motor Bus Co., Hong Kong, in 1972, it received a Gardner 6LW engine, Daimler transmission and a new KMB body.

Rhondda Transport Co. operated a small coach fleet and in 1964 replaced three Strachan-bodied Leyland Tiger Cubs with three Duple Vega Major C47F-bodied Bedford VAL14s, the first of which, 395 (395 WTG), was seen at the company's Porth depot in October 1969.

Rhondda Transport Co.'s 320 (RTG 320F), a 1968 Leyland Leopard PSU3/2R with a Willowbrook DP49F body, shows off the attractive green and cream livery the company used for its coaches and dual-purpose vehicles. When seen in Cardiff bus station in February 1972 it was carrying its new Western Welsh fleet number of 2320 as that company had absorbed Rhondda in January 1971.

South Wales Transport bought 33/4 (TCY 101/2), low-height (8-foot 11-inch) AEC Regent V 2D3RAs with Roe B37F bodywork, in 1959 for services in the Llanelli Dock area. TCY 101 was renumbered 209 in November 1970 and was seen in use as a staff bus in Oxford Street, Swansea, in February 1972.

New to small BET-group operator James of Ammanford in 1959 as fleet number 228, RTH 638, a Leyland Atlantean PDR1/1 with a Metro-Cammell L39/34F body, became South Wales Transport 1228 when the James fleet was taken over in September 1962. Seen at St Mary's, Swansea, in May 1969, it was sold to City of Oxford Motor Services in 1970.

South Wales Transport 441 (NCY 293G) was an AEC Reliance 6U2R with a Willowbrook B53F body new in September 1968 as fleet number 1962, being renumbered 441 in 1970. When seen at St Mary's, Swansea, in February 1972 it had recently been fitted with a Johnson Fare Box for trial operation on service 38 to Llansamlet.

In the early 1970s, South Wales Transport bought lightweight Bedfords and Fords. 239 (RWN 239M) was a Ford R1014 with a Willowbrook 001 B45F body, and is seen in Cardiff bus station when new in March 1974. Cardiff to Llanelli was a 55-mile journey – and this is before the M4 was completed westwards!

New to Thomas Bros, Port Talbot, in 1955, Leyland Tiger Cub PSUC1/1 PTX 202 had a Weymann B44F body. Seen at the Sandfields depot in March 1972, it retained Thomas's blue livery but with (slightly amended here!) South Wales fleet names. It went to dealer Paul Sykes at Blackerhill later the same month.

Originally United Welsh 120, 1960 ECW B45F-bodied Bristol MW6G WCY 697 became 378 in the South Wales fleet in January 1971. It carried a special low-height body to clear a low bridge at Pontrhydyfen and was seen in Swansea's bus station in March 1975, it was withdrawn in 1976 and sold in May 1977.

United Welsh number 11 (753 BWN) was a Bristol SUL4A with ECW C33F bodywork new in July 1962. Seen in Cardiff in January 1970, it became 121 in the South Wales fleet in January 1971 and was sold in 1972.

UCY 154H, a Bedford VAM70 with a Duple Viceroy C41F body, was new as United Welsh 23 in February 1970. It became 132 in the South Wales fleet in January 1971 and was picking up tour passengers in Cardiff bus station when seen in May 1973.

Seen in Cardiff bus station on its first day in service, 1 August 1977, Western Welsh HR1777 (SKG 896S) was a Bristol VRT/SL3/501 with an ECW H43/31F body. It passed to the new Red & White company in February 1991 and to Avon Fire Brigade for accident training in May 1996.

BTG 513J was ordered by the Rhondda Transport Co. but was delivered to Western Welsh as 513 after the merger. It was a Leyland Atlantean PDR1A/1 with Alexander H42/31F bodywork and was new in January 1971. It was later numbered HR271, HR5771 and finally XR1996 to reflect its highbridge body. Photographed in Aberrhondda Road, Porth, in April 1974, the erstwhile Rhondda depot was to the left of the picture.

Gwent Independent Operators

SWO 444 was a Commer Avenger IV with a Plaxton C41F body that had been new to Scout Service Station, Newbridge, in February 1958. Owned by Anstice (A&J) of Newport when photographed in Porthcawl in August 1970, it had been sold by June 1973.

Chivers of Brynmawr purchased CUJ 315C, a 1965 Bedford SB5 with a Duple Bella Vega C41F body, from Whittle, Highley, in February 1966. It was photographed in Porthcawl in August 1970. Until transferred to Gwent in the 1974 Local Government Reorganisation, the Brynmawr area was in Brecknockshire.

Cleverly (Capitol), Cwmbran, had just acquired 214 CCH, a 1963 Leyland Leopard PSU3/1R with Willowbrook DP51F bodywork, from Trent when it was seen in Cardiff in July 1978.

Contract Bus Services was the transport arm of building contractor Sir Robert McAlpine and in August 1970 was using KRN 193, a Leyland Tiger Cub PSUC1/2 with a Duple Britannia C41F body that had been new to Scout Motor Services of Preston in 1957. It was seen in the Forest of Dean, heading for its Caerwent base.

CEK 587D was a very unusual vehicle; it had a left-hand drive export Leyland Worldmaster chassis rescued from a ship which had been sunk in the River Thames and sent to Van Hool in Belgium for bodying. It and sister vehicle CEK 588D entered service with Smith, Wigan, in July 1966, and were the first Van Hool bodies in the UK. CEK 587D passed to R. I. Davies of Tredegar in July 1970, where it operated on Continental tours under the Jason Tours banner. It was seen in Cardiff's bus station in May 1971.

R. I. Davies of Tredegar must have been impressed with CEK 587D as it bought more Van Hool, bodied coaches, including YWO 490J – a C49F-bodied Ford R226 new in 1971 and seen in Porthcawl in June 1972. It was sold in 1975 and disappeared (presumed scrapped) in 1983.

R. I. Davies inherited stage carriage services in Merthyr Tydfil when it acquired Wheatsheaf Motors. OAX 415M, a Ford R226 with Willowbrook 001 B52F bodywork new in October 1973, was seen in Merthyr Tydfil bus station on the service to Trefechan the following month.

CEO 950 was a Leyland Titan PD2/40 with a Park Royal H32/28R body that was new to Barrow-in-Furness Corporation in 1958. It was sold to R. I. Davies of Tredegar in May 1975 and is also seen on the service to Trefechan. Davies sold the vehicle in March 1976.

Seen when exhibited at the 1974 Commercial Motor Show at Earls Court, this Duple Dominant C35F-bodied Bristol LHS6L was registered HAX 399N by R. I. Davies of Tredegar before entering service in January 1975. It was sold in September 1976 and is currently preserved under the registration AOR 631A.

Edmunds of Rassau, Ebbw Vale, had a liking for ECW-bodied Bristols. XNU 414 was a DP43F-bodied LS6G which had been new to Midland General in 1955 but was bought from Eastern Counties in August 1972. Seen at Edmunds's garage in April 1973, it had gone by that June.

New to Geddes (Burton Cars), Brixham, in June 1967, Plaxton Panorama C52F-bodied Bedford VAL14 JOD 529E was with Gulley's Tours of Newport when it visited Aberavon in July 1974. It was sold in April 1978.

Tredegar supported two large independent operators: R. I. Davies and Hill's. 411 AWO was a Leyland Tiger Cub PSUC1/1 with a Willowbrook B45F body that was new to the latter in May 1961. Photographed in Tredegar bus station on a wet day in February 1972, it passed to Jenkins, Capel Iwan, in November 1975.

New to Glenton Tours, London SE18, in April 1956, Plaxton C30F-bodied AEC Regal IV 9822S SLK 67 was with Howells & Withers of Pontllanfraith when seen at Barry Island in June 1968; it had been acquired from Street, Barnstaple.

Mullen of Blackwood acquired 893 ADV, a 1959 AEC Reliance 2MU3RV with Willowbrook C41F bodywork, from Court Garages, Torquay, in January 1969. Court Garages was a subsidiary of Devon General, to whom the coach had been new as TCR 893. It is seen in Sophia Gardens, Cardiff, for the Miners' Gala in June 1970.

New to Best, London W5, in August 1970, RAR 678J was a Daimler Roadliner SRP8 with a Plaxton Panorama Elite C51F body. When seen in October 1976 it was with John Nicholls of Tredegar and was sold to Green, Luddendenfoot, in October 1983.

Terry Partridge of Garndiffaith was using FYC 127C, a 1965 Bedford VAM3 with Willowbrook DP45F bodywork, in June 1974 when it was seen in Sophia Gardens, Cardiff. It had been new to Wake, Sparkford, in December 1965 and was sold on by Partridge by December 1978.

PWO 432F was new to W. G. & C. S. Peake of Pontypool in July 1968. A Ford R192 with a Duple Viceroy C45F body, it was caught in Weston-super-Mare on Bank Holiday Monday, 28 August 1972.

New as Stratford Blue number 52 in 1962, when seen in Porthcawl in August 1973 Leyland Tiger Cub 5452 WD was with W. G. & C. S. Peake of Pontypool. It had a PSUC1/1 chassis and Marshall DP41F bodywork.

C. S. Prance, using the fleet name Newport Travel Services, acquired 4068 DH, a 1964 Bedford SB5 with Plaxton Embassy C41F coachwork, from Ashley, Dawley, in July 1972. It was photographed in Aberavon the following month. C. S. Prance was also a partner in Prance's Cardiff operation.

Richards of Nantyglo used the fleet name Richards of Brynmawr. VPM 898 was a 1962 AEC Reliance 4MU3RA with Harrington Cavalier 36 C51F bodywork that was originally a Harrington demonstrator. Acquired from G & G, Leamington Spa, in August 1975, it was seen at Penpentre, near Talybont-on-Usk, in June 1977.

ADW 178K was a Willowbrook 002 Expressway C45F-bodied Bedford YRQ new to A. B. Smith of Newport in July 1972. Photographed in the coach park at Aberavon when new, it passed to Borough of Newport Transport in July 1974 and gained the fleet number 110.

Bob Truman of Pontypool acquired GNJ 839D from Henley, Abertillery, in August 1969. This Bedford J2SZ10 with a Duple Midland Compact C19F body had been new to Ives, St Leonards, in 1966. When seen in January 1974 it was parked up at the rear of Cardiff Central Station.

Acquired by Williams of Talywain in January 1973, Duple Vega C33F-bodied Bedford SB ECK 315 had been new to Scout Motor Services, Preston, in June 1951, but later spent some time with Blue Coach Tours, St Helier, Jersey, with registration J 16110. It was in Cardiff for a rugby international when seen in January 1974.

Withers Travel Ltd of Pontllanfraith, associated with Howells & Withers, purchased RBX 700 from West Wales, Tycroes, in November 1970; it was a Guy Arab IV 6LW with a Massey L34/33RD body that was new in 1958. Seen at Withers's garage in March 1972, it was sold to Towler, Elm, Cambridgeshire, in 1977.

Mid Glamorgan Independent Operators

The 36-foot Thames 676E was Ford's answer to Bedford's VAL14. Announced in 1963 and replaced by the R226 in 1965, it was quite a rare vehicle. Plaxton Panorama C52F-bodied KMT 4C was acquired by Baker (A. B. Coaches) of Gelli in the Rhondda in November 1972. It was photographed in Sophia Gardens, Cardiff, in November 1973.

S. A. Bebb of Llantwit Fardre bought PTX 995F, a Ford R192 with a Duple Viceroy C45F body, in January 1968; note the seating arrangement with tables in the centre of the coach. It was seen in Westgate Street, Cardiff, in April 1968, at which time Bebb operated around a dozen vehicles.

Carrying the S. A. Bebb International fleet name, Duple Dominant C57F-bodied
Seddon Pennine 6 NTG 4L was new in May 1973 and was in Porthcawl that August.
It was sold in August 1975 and its last road tax was surrendered in April 1989.

Seen in Sardis Road, Pontypridd, when three months old, Bebb of Llantwit Fardre's
HKG 65N was a Bristol LHS6L with a Plaxton Supreme Express C33F body and had
been new in February 1975. It carried A. B. S. (Amalgamated Bus Services) lettering.
This was used for some stage carriage services which had at one time been jointly
operated by Bebb, Edwards, Beddau and Maisey, Church Village.

Photographed at its Caerau garage in September 1975, Brewer's 433 UNY was a Leyland Leopard PSU3/3R with a Marshall B59F body and it had been bought new in July 1963. It was sold to Kenfig Motors in February 1979.

The Willowbrook 002 Expressway gained quite a following in South Wales; seen at Earls Court in September 1972, this AEC Reliance 6MU4R with C45F bodywork was registered LTX 591L by Brewer of Caerau in November 1972. It had quite a long life for an Expressway, lasting until December 1991.

Purchased by Brewer of Caerau from the City of Cardiff Transport Department in May 1976 when only eight years old, Alexander B47D-bodied AEC Swift MP2R MBO 523F lasted another eight years in this fleet, being sold for non-PSV use in December 1984.

Caerphilly Greys operated DTM 870D, a 1966 Bedford J2SZ10 with a Plaxton C20F body, from February to November 1976. It had been new to Stringer, Ampthill, but was acquired from Conwy Borough Council. Later a caravan, it was life-expired in August 1998.

Sidney Davies of Penygraig owned OBO 666M, a Bedford YRT with Duple Dominant C53F bodywork, from September 1973 to May 1977, when it was sold to Evans, Pentre Llanrhaeadr. It was life-expired in May 2002.

Edwards of Beddau bought CNY 618J, a Seddon Pennine 4 with Plaxton Panorama Elite C51F bodywork, in February 1971. It was seen in Porthcawl in June 1972. Edwards, now based in Llantrisant, is one of the largest independent operators in South Wales.

MTX 945L was a Bedford SB5 with Plaxton Panorama IV C41F coachwork new to Edwards of Beddau in March 1973. It was photographed in Porthcawl in June 1974 and ended its life as a mobile caravan from January 1993 to September 1999.

W. A. & R. Edwards of Talbot Green purchased XNY 209, a Bedford C4Z2 with a Duple C26F body, in December 1957. It was seen leaving Hensol Hospital in September 1971. Following its closure in 2003, the early eighteenth-century Hensol Castle was redeveloped as The Vale Resort – an upmarket hotel and leisure complex.

WXC 342, a Bedford SB8 with a Harrington C37F body, was new to Orange Luxury Coaches, London N16, in 1959 and had made its way to John Evans' Express Motors fleet at Kenfig Hill by June 1971, when it was in Cardiff for the Miners' Gala.

New Tredegar was in Monmouthshire in 1965 when Evans Coaches Ltd bought Plaxton Panorama C41F-bodied Bedford SB5 DAX 525C and gave it fleet number 29. Seen in Porthcawl in August 1975, it was sold to Tredegar Royals Jazz Band in 1980.

ULJ 800, an AEC Reliance MU3RA with a Plaxton Consort C41C body, had been new to Excelsior European, Bournemouth, in October 1956. Henderson of Penygraig acquired it from Reliance, Newbury, in October 1972 and gave it fleet number 11. Seen at Aberavon Beach in July 1974, it had been disposed of by October 1978.

In June 1974 Humphries Brothers of Bridgend was running NTA 935F, a Bedford VAM70 with a Duple Viceroy C45F body that had been new to Trathen, Yelverton, in 1968.

Bedford VAL14 390 GEW was fitted with a Yeates Fiesta C52F body and was acquired by D. James & Sons of Aberdare from Howells & Withers, Pontllanfraith, in August 1970. It had originated with Whippet, Hilton, Cambridgeshire, in May 1963 and was seen in Museum Avenue, Cardiff, in June 1972.

W. H. John of Coity, near Bridgend, used the fleet name Coity Motors. MUH 138 was a Leyland Tiger Cub PSUC1/1 with Weymann B44F bodywork that was new as Western Welsh 1138 in 1956. Bought by W. H. John in June 1971, it was seen at its rather remote garage in April 1974 and had been withdrawn by May 1976.

T. E. John of Tonypandy used the fleet name Gaytime Coaches and purchased UUR 104J, a 1971 Ford R192 with a Caetano Cascais C45F body, from Turner, Hitchin, in April 1973. It was seen in the coach park at Porthcawl on a sunny day in August 1973.

When built on the Ford 570E chassis, Duple's Bella Vega body was known as the Trooper. BOF 317C was new to Eatonways, Birmingham, in 1965 and when seen at Aberavon in July 1974 was owned by Fred Jones of Aberaman, who had acquired it in April 1972.

Jones Motors of Ynysybwl, a village north of Pontypridd, operated EDJ 508, a Leyland Titan PD2/20 with East Lancs H33/28R bodywork that had been new to St Helens Corporation in 1955 as number F108. Seen in Museum Avenue in Cardiff in June 1972, it had left the fleet by June 1973.

Also with Jones Motors of Ynysybwl, AHW 942B was a Bedford SB5 with a Duple (Northern) Firefly C41F body that had been new to Wessex, Bristol, in April 1964. Seen on a day tour to Doddington House in May 1975, it passed to Jenkins, Newport, Gwent, in June 1978.

TMT 763F was a significant vehicle in having the first Bristol LHL6L chassis built. Fitted with Plaxton Panorama I C53F coachwork, it had been new to Wilder, Felthan, in June 1968 and was acquired by Kenfig Motors in May 1971. It was seen in Cardiff for the Miners' Gala in June 1972.

C. R. Lewis of Maesteg, using the fleet name Lewis & Jacob, had bought 997 UTX, a Marshall B30F-bodied Bedford VAS1, in August 1963. It was photographed in a car park in its home town in March 1974.

GTX 437 was a 1947 Leyland Tiger PS1/1 with a Neath Coachbuilders B39F body that served with Llynfi Motors of Maesteg as fleet number 37 until 1983. Originally carrying a Massey body, it received this new body in 1957. Sold for preservation, it was seen in Swansea in June 1998.

Llynfi Motors of Maesteg bought 66 (OTC 738) from Leyland Motors in March 1955. New in June 1952, it had the first Tiger Cub chassis and a Saunders-Roe B44F body and was still in use when seen at the depot in September 1975.

New to AEC, Southall, in December 1953 as a demonstrator, 210 AMP was a Monocoach with Park Royal B44F bodywork. It became Llynfi of Maesteg's number 67 in December 1955. Photographed at the depot in March 1974, it had gone by October 1978.

4777 NE was a Leyland Leopard L2T chassis with a Burlingham Seagull 70 C41F body that showed distinct transatlantic influence. New to Spencer, Manchester, in 1962, it became Llynfi of Maesteg's 102 in March 1967.

Llynfi of Maesteg's 117 (NTX 595L) was a Plaxton Derwent DP45F-bodied Bristol LH6L that was new in April 1973. Seen in Cardiff in June 1974, it passed with the Llynfi business to Brewer in July 1988.

A popular coach chassis in the 1950s and early 1960s was the Leyland Tiger Cub. BHB 361 was a PSUC1/2 version with a Duple Britannia C43F body and was new to Morlais of Merthyr Tydfil in June 1960. Seen at its Traction Yard garage in April 1973, Morlais had ceased operations by October 1978.

Carrying Morlais of Merthyr Tydfil's later cream and yellow livery, JHB 500L was a Ford R192 with Willowbrook 002 Expressway C45F coachwork and was photographed at Aust Services on the M4 when new in August 1972. It later operated for Bernard Kavanagh of Urlingford in the Republic of Ireland.

In late 1969 Morris of Pencoed acquired 1175–7 CD, 1960 Albion Aberdonian MR11Ls with Harrington Cavalier C41F bodies, from Charlies Cars of Bournemouth. 1175 CD was seen out of use at the garage in March 1972 and had gone by May 1973.

Morris of Pencoed bought LGG 761E from Davis, Hamilton, in November 1971. An AEC Reliance 590 2U3RA with Alexander Y-type C49F body, it had been new to the Scottish Co-operative Wholesale Society, Glasgow, in April 1967. It was photographed at Morris's Pencoed garage in March 1972.

Morris of Pencoed purchased PWB 949E, a 1967 Ford R226 with a Willowbrook 001 DP49F body, from Booth & Fisher, Halfway, near Sheffield. It was seen in Sophia Gardens, Cardiff, in June 1974 and had left the fleet by October 1978.

New to Morris of Pencoed in September 1976, NUH 883R had a Bedford YMT chassis and an Irish-built Van Hool-McArdle C53F body. Photographed in Cardiff in June 1977, it was sold in March 1978 and later became a car transporter until its road tax expired at the end of February 2010.

New to London Transport in 1952 as RT3456, AEC Regent III LYR 875 originally had a Weymann body but received this Saunders H30/26R body on final overhaul in August 1965. Porthcawl Omnibus Company acquired it in June 1970 and it was seen at its Kenfig Hill garage in April 1973 accompanied by similar KGK 673 (ex-RT1204) and former Cardiff Leyland Titan PD2A XUH 371.

Porthcawl Omnibus Co. bought NHE 114, a 1958 Leyland Tiger Cub PSUC1/1T with a Park Royal B44F body, from Yorkshire Traction in May 1972. Freshly prepared for service, it was seen at the Kenfig Hill garage in April 1973. At this time Porthcawl Omnibus Company and Kenfig Motors were associated fleets.

RNY 453M was a Bedford YRT with a Willowbrook 002 Expressway C51F body and was new in November 1973 to the Porthcawl Omnibus Company. Seen in one of the town's car parks in June 1974, it lasted long enough to be transferred to Williams, Porthcawl, in October 1990.

The Rhymney area was in Monmouthshire until April 1974, when it became part of Mid Glamorgan. Rhymney Transport Services bought Bedford YRT TTG 170M, which had a Duple Dominant Express C53F body and was new in July 1974. It was covered in snow when seen in Merthyr Tydfil in November 1977.

Still operating for Samuel & Mason of Hirwaun in August 1969 when seen at Barry Island, DHL 846 was a Commer Avenger I with Plaxton C33F body that had been new to Cawthorne, Barugh, in November 1951. It was out of use by January 1973.

In June 1976 D. W. Thomas of Tonteg was operating KJC 686, a Commer Avenger IV with Duple Corinthian C41F body that had been new to Red Garages, Llandudno, in May 1962. Photographed in Sophia Gardens, Cardiff, for the annual South Wales Miners' Gala, it later passed to James, Cardiff.

Waddon of Caerphilly was well-known for Continental tours and JWO 179P, a Bedford YRT with a Plaxton Supreme C53F body, was photographed carrying Waddon's International lettering when new in April 1976. It had been sold by April 1981.

John Williams of Porthcawl bought Bedford YRQ JTG 999K new in June 1972. It had a Duple Viceroy Express C45F body. Photographed in Sophia Gardens, Cardiff, in November 1973, it had left the fleet by February 1979.

Mrs E. M. Williams of Treorchy operated as Victoria Motorways and bought DKG 888L in May 1973. It was a Volvo B58-56 with Duple Dominant C51F bodywork and, after sale by Williams in 1983, it was reregistered PNH 184 and then SBF 210L. It was in Cardiff for a rugby international in February 1975.

South Glamorgan Independent Operators

New to Byng, Portsmouth, in June 1962, Bedford VAS1 500 ABK had made its way to C. K. Coaches of Cardiff by March 1976. It had a twenty-nine-seat Duple Bella Vista body and later operated for Holden, Dudley, before becoming a store shed in Wallasey in 1980. C. K. Coaches was owned by Carole and Keith Morris, and ceased operations in July 1988.

C. K. Coaches of Cardiff bought Alexander-bodied Leyland Atlantean PDR1/1 AGA 116B from Morris, Pencoed, in January 1978; it had been new to Glasgow as LA177 in 1964. In July 1978 it was operating a rail replacement service from Cardiff Central station.

Also operated by C. K. Coaches of Cardiff, Park Royal H47/33D-bodied 33-foot
Daimler Fleetline CRG6LX SOE 917H had come from West Midlands PTE (where
it was numbered 3917) in June 1979. It was photographed in the industrial Curran
Road the following month.

PEP 380 was a Bedford SB5 with Yeates Fiesta 44 bodywork that was new to Mid
Wales Motorways, Newtown, in April 1963. It was notable in squeezing fifty-three
bus seats (in a 3+2 layout) into the body. It passed to Grove of Barry in September
1970 and was burnt out in August 1979. It was photographed near Grove's Barry
garage in April 1974.

OUP 650D was an AEC Reliance 4MU3RA with a Plaxton Highway DP51F body that had been new to O. K. Motor Services, Bishop Auckland, in May 1966. Acquired by Grove Coach Hire of Barry in November 1973, it was photographed in April 1974. Grove was renamed Coastal Continental in 1976 and OUP 650D continued to serve until September 1985.

Plaxton Panorama C51F-bodied Daimler Roadliner SRC6 MDH 212E was new to Central, Walsall, in May 1967. By August 1971, when it was seen in Porthcawl, it was with Croft Coaches of Roath, Cardiff, but had gone by January 1973.

Duple Viceroy C53F-bodied Ford R226 YKG 338K was new to Croft Coaches of Roath, Cardiff, in April 1972 and was seen in Aberavon in July 1974. It later passed to James, Cardiff.

Falconer & Watts of Llanishen, Cardiff, bought Bedford VAS5 CKG 470L new in January 1973 and had it fitted with a Duple Vista 25 C29F body. It was seen in Central Square, Cardiff, in September 1973.

G. R. Lang of Gabalfa, Cardiff, ran as Castle Coaches and bought Ford R1114 HNY 602N, fitted with a smart Caetano Estoril II C53F body, in March 1975. Seen at Sophia Gardens, Cardiff, in June 1976, it had left the fleet by October 1981.

In August 1975, Pearce of Cardiff was operating 978 HHT, a 1960 Bedford SB1 with a Duple Vega C41F body that had been new to Wessex, Bristol. Some years after sale by Pearce it became a car transporter, reregistered as AAX 551A, and was defunct by October 1988.

In July 1974, Powell of Cardiff was operating 6 DON, a Ford 570E with Harrington Crusader C41F coachwork that had been new to Burley, Birmingham, in May 1961. Powell had ceased operating by October 1978.

R. R. & C. S. Prance of Cardiff was running 169 BUP in May 1971. It was an Albion Aberdonian MR11L with Willowbrook B45F bodywork that had been new to Venture Travel, Consett, County Durham, in 1959 as fleet number 169. It was seen near Prance's Godfrey Street garage.

In January 1973, R. R. & C. S. Prance of Cardiff purchased KYD 151, a 1949 AEC Regal III with a Harrington dorsal fin C33F body, and operated it as a semi-preserved coach. It was on a day trip to the Kennet & Avon Canal when photographed at Honey Street in July 1973. Later sold for preservation, it still exists, although the road tax expired in August 1982.

New as a demonstrator for dealer Arlington at Potters Bar in November 1970, RAR 689J was a Bedford VAM70 with a Van Hool Vistadome C45F body that had made its way to the R. R. & C. S. Prance of Cardiff fleet by March 1974, when it was seen in that city's Queen Street. Van Hool only bodied two Bedford VAM70 chassis before that model was superseded by the YRQ.

Retter (Fairtax) of Cardiff was a short-lived operator which operated 6002 BT – a 1961 Bedford SB1 with a Plaxton Embassy C41F body – as fleet number 3 in August 1971. It originated with Boddy, Bridlington, and was later re-registered 485 OZI with Stewart, Dublin.

W. F. Sing of Grangetown, Cardiff, adopted the grand title of Cardiff Motorways and purchased WKG 136, a 1961 AEC Reliance 2MU3RA with a Weymann C36F body, from Western Welsh in October 1970. Seen near Sing's Grangetown base in May 1971, WKG 136 was sold to Thomas (Airport Coaches), Rhoose, in October of that year.

Duple Viscount C45F-bodied Ford R192 MYY 992D was new to Dix, Dagenham, in 1966 and by May 1971 had found its way to W. F. Sing's Cardiff Motorways fleet. Sold by January 1973, it was later a mobile caravan until its road tax expired in September 1992.

JWO 31D was a Ford R226 with a Duple Mariner C52F body that had been new to R. I. Davies, Tredegar, in June 1966. When seen in Sophia Gardens, Cardiff, in June 1976 it was with the Taurus Travel fleet of M. K. Stevens of Pentrebane, Cardiff. Note the different side window arrangement compared to the Viscount body on Sing's MYY 992D.

Thomas Motors of Barry bought ATG 708J, a Willowbrook B53F-bodied Leyland Leopard PSU3A/4R that was new in August 1970. It could usually be found on the 304 service between Cardiff and Barry via Dinas Powis, which was operated jointly with Western Welsh.

Sid Thomas of Rhoose used the fleet name Airport Coaches and in April 1974 was operating LMP 977K, a Seddon Pennine 6 with a Caetano Lisboa C57F body that had been new to Wilder, Feltham, in 1972. Thomas sold this coach in April 1977.

Carrying an angular Reeve Burgess seventeen-seat body, Bedford CF340 TTX 137S was new to N. C. Venn of Cardiff in October 1977. Caught outside the owner's premises in Fairwater in August 1978, it was sold by January 1982, and exported in March 1988.

Very few Unicar bodies were sold in the United Kingdom, one being CTG 526V – a C53F-bodied Bedford YMT that was new to N. C. Venn of Cardiff in September 1979. It was seen at Garden Festival Wales in Ebbw Vale in May 1992 and was sold to dealer Wacton at Bromyard in February 1996.

West Glamorgan Independent Operators

Cream Line Services Ltd of Tonmawr used the fleet name Creamline and purchased GNY 715K, a Leyland Leopard PSU3B/4R with a Plaxton Panorama Elite I C53F body that was new in December 1971. When photographed in February 1972 it was in Cardiff for a rugby international. Sold in February 1987, its engine failed in 1992 while being used for humanitarian aid to Romania.

Although new to Ribble as 1027 in 1961, Cream Line of Tonmawr acquired Harrington Cavalier C41F-bodied Leyland Leopard L2 PCK 609 from Cumberland, where it had been numbered 1300, in May 1973. Photographed in Cardiff in November 1973, it lasted with Cream Line until June 1978.

Cream Line of Tonmawr acquired Leyland Titan PD2/27 PFR 350 from Blackpool Corporation in September 1975. It had a Metro-Cammell FH35/26R body and had been new in April 1959. Photographed at the Tonmawr garage when newly prepared for service, it was sold in August 1978.

D Coaches of Morriston bought Bristol LD6G 845 AFM from Cream Line, Tonmawr, in August 1973. New to Crosville as MG 888 (later DLG 888) in 1957, platform doors were fitted to its ECW H33/27R body in 1963 and it was sold to Cream Line in May 1972. Seen in Cathedral Road, Cardiff, in June 1974, it lasted with D Coaches until late 1976.

New as Birch Bros' K62 in June 1970, BUL 62H later ran in the Grey Green fleet of the Ewer Group. A Seddon Pennine 4 with a Plaxton Panorama Elite C45F body, it was sold to D Coaches of Morriston in October 1974. Seen in Cardiff in June 1976, it served D Coaches until September 1984.

D Coaches of Morriston bought Duple Dominant C45F-bodied Bedford YRQ PWN 522M, which was new in January 1974. It was seen in a very muddy Sophia Gardens, Cardiff, in the same month.

Entering service in December 1956 as Edinburgh Corporation 750, Leyland Titan PD2/20 NSF 750 had a Metro-Cammell H34/29R body. It passed to Lothian in May 1975 and was acquired by D Coaches of Morriston in February 1976. Looking very smart in this August 1980 view at D Coaches' depot, it was withdrawn in June 1981. It is flanked by LWS 523 and ASC 674B, both of which were also originally Edinburgh buses.

Davies of Cwmgwrach, a village near Glyn Neath, acquired 862 HAL – an AEC Reliance 2MU3RV with a Plaxton Panorama C41F body – from Baker, Ferndale, in September 1974. It was seen in Cardiff for the Miners' Gala in June 1976. It had been new to Barton, Chilwell, as 862 in December 1960.

New to Owen, Upper Boddington, Northamptonshire, Hutchins of Pontardawe acquired BJF 334B – a 1964 Bedford VAS1 with a Plaxton Embassy C29F body – by November 1973, when it was seen in Cardiff. Sold to Fussell, Swansea, in 1978, and later operating with a jazz band in Caerphilly, it was taxed until 30 April 1999.

Brian Isaac of Landore acquired NTX 408L in 1978 and numbered it 19. It was a Bedford YRT with a Duple Dominant C53F body that had been new to Morris, Pencoed, in May 1973, and when photographed in August 1980 it had just been acquired by D Coaches, Morriston.

Jenkins of Penclawdd on the Gower Peninsula used the fleet name Hillside Motors and had purchased 332 FTM from Waters, Addlestone, in October 1970. It was a Ford 570E with a Burlingham Gannet C41F body that had been new to Ludlow, Birmingham, in April 1962. It was seen in Sophia Gardens, Cardiff, in June 1973.

Jenkins of Skewen gave fleet number 9 to YUD 585, a 1963 Bedford VAS1 with Plaxton Embassy C29F body bought from Seward, Dalwood, Devon, in November 1969. It was seen at the garage in March 1974.

Jenkins of Skewen's fleet number 20 was ECW C33F-bodied Bristol SC4LK 802 FFM, which had started life as Crosville's CSG622 in March 1958, passing to Jenkins in December 1970. It was seen at the garage in March 1974 and was withdrawn in January 1976.

Caught at Jenkins of Skewen's garage soon after delivery in March 1974 (note the Plaxton poster in the side window), RCY 843M was a Plaxton Panorama Elite III C53F-bodied Ford R226. It passed to Chapman, Airdrie, in December 1981.

R. J. Jones & Sons of Clydach (north-east of Swansea) acquired TXJ 700, a 1957 Bedford SBG with a Duple Super Vega C41F body, from Castle, Llandovery, in November 1971. It was in Cardiff for the June 1974 Miners' Gala.

The 1975 Miners' Gala saw Jones of Clydach's XTH 10 in Cardiff. This was a Bedford SB8 with Burlingham Seagull C41F bodywork bought from West Wales, Tycroes, the previous February. It retained its West Wales fleet number of 43.

I. Jones of Pontardawe used the Glantawe Coaches fleet name and acquired Ford R226 TFA 226J from Viking, Woodville, in November 1974. New in April 1971, it had a Duple Viceroy C45F body. I caught up with it in Porthcawl in May 1975 and it was sold in July 1987.

Morris Bros of Swansea had a liking for the ECW-bodied Bristol product and many second-hand examples were bought, including LD6G UHY 410, which had a H33/25RD body. It came from the Bristol Omnibus Co. fleet, where it was numbered L8281, in 1971. It was seen on St Helens Road, Swansea, in March 1974.

New to Morris Bros of Swansea in April 1972, ECY 2K was a Bedford YRQ with a Plaxton Panorama Elite C45F body. It was seen in Abergavenny that September and lasted to pass to Cleverly, Cwmbran, with the Morris business in May 1984.

I did not take much interest in minibuses in the 1970s, but HCY 8L – Morris Bros of Swansea's 1972 diesel-engined long-wheelbase Ford Transit twelve-seater – did catch my eye at Sophia Gardens, Cardiff, in January 1974.

Nelson of Glynneath acquired NDH 449E, a 1967 Ford R192 with a Duple Bella Venture C45F body, from Prance, Cardiff, in November 1972. It had been new to Mason, Darlaston, in March 1967 and it was seen in Sophia Gardens, Cardiff, for the June 1973 Miners' Gala.

Pritchard of Resolven was operating MHX 912C, a Bedford SB13 with Harrington Crusader C41F coachwork, when it was seen in Cardiff in June 1976. It had been new to Thomas, West Ewell, in April 1965 and went from Pritchard to Warren, Neath, by February 1977.

Garnswllt is a rural village near the Swansea/Carmarthen border and was the home of Peter Smith, who bought LNY 176L – a Ford R192 with a Willowbrook 002 Expressway C45F body – new in August 1972. The operator became Triafon Motors in 1975 and Pathlin in 1976, but ceased operations in 1977. LNY 176L was seen in Sophia Gardens, Cardiff, for the June 1974 Miners' Gala.

D. J. Thomas of Neath Abbey bought 878 HMJ, a Ford 570E with a Duple Thames Trooper C41F body, from Dodsworth, Minskip, in February 1969. It had been new to Wells, Hatfield Peverel, in March 1963 and it was seen in Sophia Gardens, Cardiff, in June 1973.

H. L. Williams of Gwaun-Cae-Gurwen used the fleet name Amman Valley Coaches and was operating YWR 95, a Ford 570E with Burlingham C41F coachwork, when it was seen in Cardiff for the June 1971 Miners' Gala. It had been new to Mosley, Barugh Green, in the West Riding of Yorkshire in July 1959.

Also at Sophia Gardens, Cardiff, in June 1971 was H. L. Williams of Gwaun-Cae-Gurwen's UHA 233, a 1954 BMMO CL3 that was rebuilt and rebodied with a Plaxton Panorama C36F body in 1962 by its original owner – the Birmingham & Midland Motor Omnibus Co. (Midland Red). It was sold to Fussell, Swansea, in July 1971.

Non-PSV Operators

New to Monmouthshire County Council in September 1972, Bedford VAS5 FWO 372L passed to Gwent County Council Social Services Department in April 1974. It was fitted with a Strachan B16FL body and was based in Pontypool, where it was photographed in September 1977.

Newport County Borough Council Social Services Department bought CDW 654L, a Sparshatt-bodied Leyland Terrier, in January 1973, and it was photographed in its home town that August. It passed to Gwent County Council in April 1974, but in February 1976 I saw it in Caerphilly with Mid Glamorgan CC Social Services. By 1995 it was noted as a mobile caravan.

Hobbs Quarries of Porthcawl acquired Albion Nimbus WKG 35, an NS3AN with Weymann DP30F bodywork, in 1975. It had been new as Western Welsh 35 in May 1961; note that the original curved driver's windscreen has been replaced by flat glass. Caught in Tonyrefail in July 1976, it was sold in January 1980.

Owned by Porthcawl Recreations in June 1972, Guy Arab LUF LCY 779 had a Park Royal C41C body and had been new to Neath & Cardiff Luxury Coaches Ltd in April 1955. Latterly painted in the desert sand and red livery, it was replaced in the N&C fleet by a second-hand AEC Reliance in 1966. It went for scrap in October 1973.

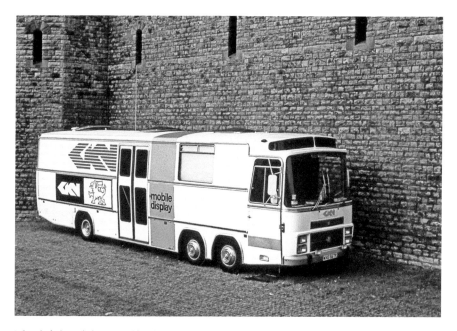

This left-hand drive Bedford VAL70 (with a Van Hool Vistadome body that was fitted out by Coventry Steel Caravans as an exhibition unit) originated with the George Kent Group in London in October 1970, where it was registered KNT 1. It was later re-registered MXE 667K and in 1975 was acquired by GKN Rolled & Bright Steel of Cardiff. It was parked up at Cardiff Castle in August 1979.

Seen in Tonypandy in June 1977, PCY 286R was an ex-Ministry of Defence Bedford SB with a Strachan body. It was operated by Scott, a contractor from Port Talbot. I have not managed to trace any further details of this bus.

New to Scout Motor Services, Preston, in August 1948, Duple-bodied Bedford OB CCK 486 was still going strong as a mobile shop when seen in March 1974. It was owned by A. Thomas of Skewen, who had acquired it from Davies (D Coaches), Morriston, sometime before March 1971.

Three vehicles await their fate at Bill Way's Cardiff East Dock scrapyard on New Year's Day 1973: VEH 584, an AEC Reliance MU3RV with a Weymann body from John Williams, Porthcawl; MDL 899, a Bedford SBG with Duple coachwork from Dolan (Shamrock), Newport; and VVH 348, a Hanson-rebuild with a Roe body from Porthcawl Omnibus Co.